Deep Down Underground

Contents	Page

written by John Lockyer

Mining has been important work ever since people found uses for the materials they discovered in the ground. In ancient times, people dug up stone for buildings. They used iron for weapons, and they made jewellery from gold and silver. Today, we still mine those materials as well as many others, including valuable gemstones like diamonds and solid fuels like coal.

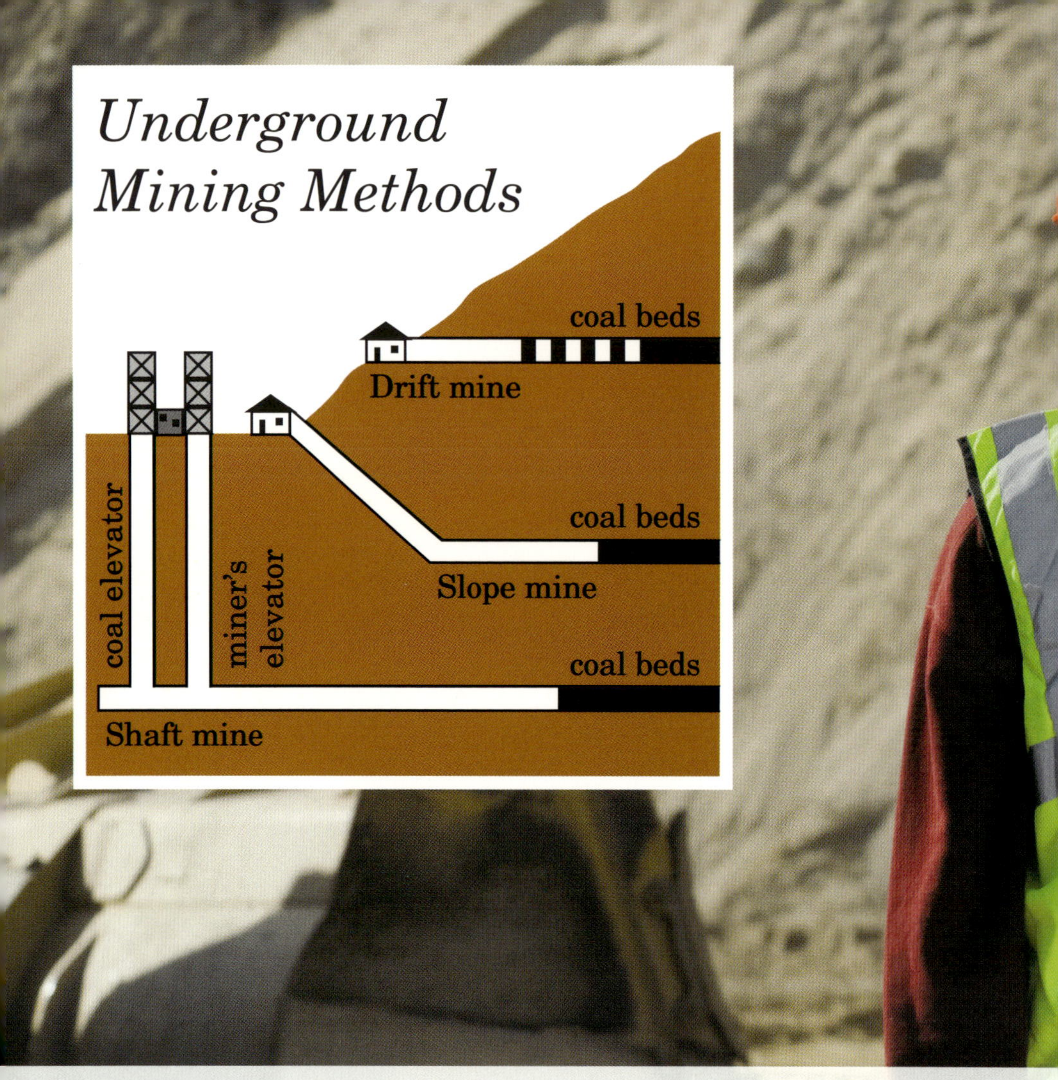

Scientists and engineers are always looking for new deposits of rocks, minerals and gemstones. When one is found, they work out how much there is and what is the best way to excavate it. Underground mining is often the safest, cheapest and least wasteful way of getting materials from the earth. There are many different ways to mine underground.

Shaft mines

A shaft mine is the deepest type of underground mine. Some shaft
mines can be almost 2½ miles /4 kilometres deep. This sort of mine
is often used to excavate coal. Three shafts are dug vertically into
the ground. Miners use one shaft. Another shaft is for transporting
machinery and minerals. The third shaft is for fresh air.
A short horizontal tunnel is dug from the bottom of the shafts to
the coal. Miners and machines reach the coal by deepening and
widening the tunnel.

Gold, silver, iron, copper, zinc, nickel and tin are known as hard minerals. They are found in rocks called ore. The ore can be mined using the hard rock mining system. A shaft is dug vertically into the ground. At different depths down the shaft, horizontal tunnels are dug out. The ore is excavated from the tunnels and brought to the surface in shuttle cars and elevators. Crushing machines separate the minerals from the ore.

Borehole mining

Borehole mining is a safe and environment-friendly way to mine gold and diamonds. A movable machine drills a hole down to the minerals or gemstones. A tube-tool is dropped into the hole. The tool forces water around the dirt, rocks and minerals. This makes a slurry, which is pumped up to a storage tank. After the water is drained off, the gold and diamonds are found in the sediment.

Drift mining is used when coal, gold or zinc are buried on the side of a mountain. The tunnels, called drifts, are dug horizontally. Usually, the opening to the mine is dug lower than the ore or mineral. This makes it easier for shuttle cars and trucks to bring the material out because they are moving downhill.

Slope mines aren't deep. They are used to excavate rocks like coal that are buried under hills or mountains. A sloping tunnel is dug down to a coal bed. After the coal is cut out of the bed it is dropped onto a conveyor which brings the rock out of the mine.

Coal mining

Underground mining machines have made miners' work easier.
Many coal mines use a long-wall cutter machine. It spins along the
mine wall, cutting out long sections of coal. After the coal drops
onto a conveyor, the machine moves forward automatically to cut
out a new section. A huge, fitted steel roof protects the cutter and
miners from falling coal.

Dump trucks

Some of the biggest trucks in the world are mine dump trucks. The wheels can be twice as tall as the drivers, so they have to climb a ladder to reach the cab. Dump trucks are used to shift large amounts of rock, dirt and minerals. Articulated dump trucks are used inside mines because they can turn around in very small spaces.

LPAK
56
6

Mining machinery

Wheel loaders, excavators, bulldozers and motor graders are used in and around mines, too. One of the world's largest machines is a coal shovel called a dragline. It weighs more than 35,000 tons. Instead of a steering wheel or levers, the operator uses a computer to work the machine.

Environment protection

Our modern world needs the materials that we dig from
the earth. But mining can pollute, change and destroy the
environment. Today, in many countries, mining companies have
to show how they are going to protect the soil, water, air, plants
and animals before they start digging. They must also show how
they are going to return the environment to its natural state
once the mining has finished.